Colonial
Places

Sarah Howarth

The Millbrook Press
Brookfield, Connecticut

For Betty and Tony

Published in the United States in 1994 by

The Millbrook Press
2 Old New Milford Road
Brookfield, Connecticut 06804

First published in Great Britain in 1994 by

Simon & Schuster Young Books
Campus 400
Maylands Avenue
Hemel Hempstead
Hertfordshire HP2 7EZ

Designed by Neil Adams
Illustrations by Philip McNeill

Text copyright © 1994 by Sarah Howarth
Illustrations copyright © 1994 by Philip McNeill

Typeset by DP Press Ltd, Sevenoaks, Kent

Printed and bound by Proost International Book Co., Belgium

Library of Congress Cataloging-in-Publication Data
Howarth, Sarah.
    Colonial places / Sarah Howarth.
        p.   cm. — (People and places)
    Includes bibliographical references and index.
    summary:
    A description of thirteen places around which life in America revolved and
    how they fit into society.
    ISBN 1-56294-513-0
    1. United States—Social life and customs—To 1775—Juvenile literature.
    2. United States—Description and travel—Juvenile literature. [1. United
    States—Social life and customs—To 1775. 2. United States—Description and
    travel.] I. Title.   II Series: Howarth, Sarah. People and places.
    E162.H69 1994b
    973—dc20   94-25754
                                                                              CIP
                                                                              AC

Picture acknowledgments

Picture research by Donna Thynne

The publishers would like to thank the following for their permission to
reproduce copyright material:
The Bettmann Archive, New York: p 16; The Bridgeman Art Library: pp 6, 10, 22,
43; A.C. Cooper: pp 3,7; E.T Archive: pp 23, 24; Kevin Fleming: p 44; Library of
Congress, Washington D.C.: p 13; The Linnean Society/Eileen Tweedy: p 19; The
Mansell Collection: pp 8, 37, 45; National Gallery of Art, Washington D.C.: p 18
(gift of Edgar William and Bernice Chrysler Garbisch); Peter Newark/Western
Americana: pp 5, 12, 29, 32; New York Historical Society: pp 14, 25; New York
Public Library: pp 17, 21, 27, 28, 33, 38, 39, 41, 42; Picture Cube Inc, Boston: pp
26, 30; The Colonial Williamsburg Foundation: p 15; Worcester Art Museum,
Worcester, Massachusetts: pp 9, 31; Zefa Picture Library: p 11.

CONTENTS

INTRODUCTION

In 1969 American astronauts landed on the moon. They were the first to do this, and people the world over felt a great sense of adventure and discovery. Many years before, in the fifteenth and sixteenth centuries, people in Europe had a similar feeling. It was the exploration of America that caused such excitement then.

To Europeans, America was a "New World," and as the first travelers' tales reached them, the excitement was as great as if people had reached the moon.

Settlements sprang up in North America as people from Europe decided to try their luck in the New World and make a home there. In this book you can visit all sorts of places that made up this American way of life, from the hunting trail to the cornfield. The book will tell you where the settlers lived, about the towns and houses they built, and how they worked and made money. You can find out where the settlers worshipped God; where they made friends and fought their enemies. The book will also tell you about the Native Americans and their encounters with the settlers.

THE COLONY

In the city of London, England, in 1630, a group of men were at work printing a new book. Written by a clergyman named Francis Higginson (1587–1630), it described a place about which the people of Europe had until recently known nothing at all: America. Higginson described America enthusiastically:

The richness of the soil here is a marvellous thing. It is hardly to be believed how well our cows, goats, horses and hogs like this country.

Claiming land in the New World

After 1492, when an expedition led by the Italian, Christopher Columbus (*c.* 1445–1506), landed in the Bahamas, European kings and queens were eager to conquer land in the Americas and claim it as their own. Land that was conquered in this way became a "colony." A colony is a place ruled by the people of a different country.

Three countries in particular claimed land in the New World: Spain, France, and Britain. Spain claimed all North America—but few Spanish people went to

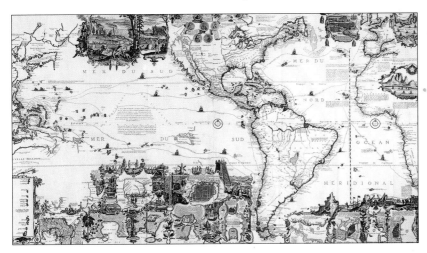

A *map of the Americas. The prospect of setting up home here attracted settlers from Britain, France, the Netherlands, and other countries.*

7

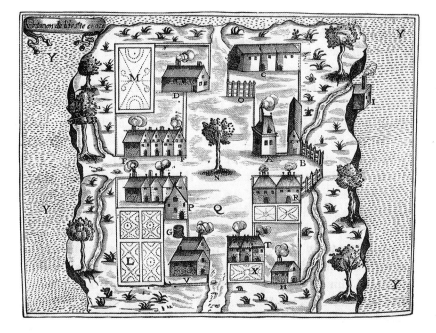

French interest in North America dated from the early 1500s. This picture was drawn to show the earliest French settlement in Acadia (present-day Nova Scotia). As well as exploring areas such as this in the north, the French were also interested in land to the south, in Florida.

settle there. France claimed Canada as a colony and was hungry for its trade in fish and furs; but, like Spain, it sent few settlers. Britain, on the other hand, set up 13 colonies along America's Atlantic coast. These soon became thriving settler communities.

There was fierce rivalry between Spain, France, and Britain. Each of these countries wanted to build up a mighty empire with many colonies. Gradually Britain won this race for an empire, and by the middle of the eighteenth century it controlled most of the eastern part of North America.

Making a new home

During the seventeenth century, a growing number of people wanted to go to America to make a new home there. One of the most famous groups to do this was the "Pilgrims," who sailed from England in 1620 in a ship named the *Mayflower*. Settlers like the Pilgrims and Francis Higginson, the clergyman described at the start of this chapter, began to set up colonies in America.

Many of these very first settlers came from England.

They were used to thinking of England as "home," and in many ways they tried to model their new way of life on the ways they had known there. During the eighteenth century, this pattern changed. There were more settlers from other countries, such as Ireland, Scotland, France, Germany, and the Netherlands. They brought new ideas and new influences to shape life in the colonies. As time went by, their ties with the "Old World" of Europe became less and less strong.

At sea with pots, pans, and poultry

Preparing to live in the "New World" of America was a big undertaking. The first settlers had to take everything they needed with them. They had to make lists of what to take in advance, and each item was carefully stowed aboard ship. *"100 waistcoats of green cotton, 100 black hats, 200 dozen hooks and eyes, 50 mats, potatoes, hemp seed, turkeys, pewter bottles, ladles, spoons"* were among the goods to be sent to the colony at Massachusetts Bay in 1629. As Francis Higginson pointed out to his readers, *"When you leave England you will find no shop to provide what you need—neither in the great ocean, nor when you come to land."*

Here we come face to face with two early settlers: a lady called Elizabeth Freake and her baby daughter, Mary. Their picture was painted in the town of Boston during the 1670s.

"Not as we did expect"

It was difficult for people in Europe to understand that in America conditions would be completely different from those they were used to. *"The country is not as we did expect,"* sighed one settler in a letter home. The first to arrive had to clear the ground, build shelters, and somehow make sure they had enough to eat. After a long, cramped, uncomfortable journey aboard ship, many people were ill when they reached land, too weak for the urgent tasks awaiting them. *"Here have died of the scurvy and the burning fever two hundred,"* wrote a man at Massachusetts Bay.

THE GOVERNOR'S HOUSE

One especially important house had to be built in each British colony: a house for the leader of the colony—the governor. A newcomer describing his first sight of America gives us a glimpse of just such a house:

When we first came here, we found about ten houses, and a fair house, newly built, for the governor.

At the governor's house

The governor was a powerful figure in each colony. He was responsible for the way the people were ruled. In the early days of the colonies, there were rarely special offices for the governor and the people who helped him. The governor and his men worked at home instead. Here they wrote letters, held meetings, and made important decisions. They debated anything and everything, from how the settlers should treat the Native

The signing of the Declaration of Independence in 1776 was a historic moment in the story of North America. The Declaration proclaimed that the American colonies were free from British control and masters of their own destiny. The British government, represented by local governors, finally had no say in the destiny of the Americas.

Americans, to where houses should be built and how much land each settler should have, to how much money craftsmen should charge for their work and what the price of food should be. Law and order, religion, education—all these issues and more were dealt with at the governor's house.

Interruptions

For the governor and his officials, doing business at home sometimes involved unexpected disruption. Interruptions from a noisy family, for example, added to the work load. This is what one man, who served as the governor of Massachusetts in the seventeenth century, had to say about trying to work at home:

I have yet no table, nor other room to write in than by the fireside upon my knee. My family come in, breaking good manners. They make me sometimes forget what I would say.

Orders from the Old World

Although the governor of a British colony had many powers, he did not rule the people single-handedly. There were other people with a share in the government. The king or queen of England, and the Parliament, had to be consulted on many matters, such as foreign trade, law, and religion. But very often the government in London was too concerned with problems of its own to pay much attention to the colonies in America. This was especially true in the middle of the seventeenth century, when disagreements between King Charles I and Parliament exploded into open war in England in 1642. At times like these, few orders were sent on the 3,000-mile journey to the colonies. The governors and their assistants became used to making their own decisions and acting independently.

The governors of the first British colonies had to make do with very basic working conditions. By the eighteenth century, the story was different. The handsome governor's palace in Williamsburg, Virginia, which is shown here, dates from this time.

Political protest in the British colonies grew after George III became king in 1760. Here a contemporary cartoon tells us about that protest. It shows a much-hated law called the Stamp Act being buried.

Speaking out in the New World

The settlers, too, had a share in the government. It soon became the custom in the British colonies for special meetings called "assemblies" to be held. Here the governor met with the people. Together they made laws and debated the colony's future. Only a few men were chosen to attend the assembly. They were expected to think not of their own interests, but to represent the interests of their neighbors. The first assembly to be held in the American colonies was held in the church at Jamestown, Virginia, in 1619. In each colony, the assembly had its own name and its own special rules for voting. In Virginia, for example, the assembly was called the House of Burgesses, and a man had to own a certain amount of land before he was permitted to vote.

Not everyone in the colonies had the right to vote on questions of politics. Women, for instance, were not permitted to vote in elections. But an important beginning was being made, for more people in America had the right to vote than in the Old World. In the Old World, politics were only for the wealthy. In America, the seeds of a new, freer, way of thinking about politics were being sown. The political system in America today traces its roots from this time.

THE CORNFIELD

One day in 1756, a man named Landon Carter sat down with a pen and paper. He was going to keep a diary of everything that happened on his plantations (estates) in Virginia. This is one of his entries:

Began to plow for oats this day. The cornfield not quite finished.

Starving times

The first settlers to arrive in America faced urgent problems. Finding food was one of the most pressing, and conditions in some colonies soon became desperate. A settler who sailed from England to Roanoke Island, off Virginia, in 1585 reported that newcomers there had supplies for only 20 days when they landed. At Jamestown in Virginia, the first settlers faced a *"starving time"* before they began to plant and harvest crops. Many people at Jamestown died of disease and hunger in the winter of 1609–1610.

A farmer harvesting the crops. The work was very hard but even the youngest children helped in the fields.

It took time for some of the settlers to realize how their very survival depended on growing enough food. Captain John Smith, one of the first leaders in Virginia, described how some newcomers were simply not interested in farming. They had arrived in the New World hoping to find gold and become rich overnight. From these people there was *"no talk, no work, but gold … gold … gold."* Captain Smith tried to change these feelings and ordered the settlers to plant corn.

"Instruments from God"

Although America was a new world to the European settlers, the land was already inhabited when they arrived. It was the home of Native Americans, whom the newcomers called "Indians." The Native Americans helped the newcomers in many ways. They traded food and shared their knowledge of local plants. In Virginia, Captain Smith recorded how they brought corn for the Europeans. Settlers at Plymouth in New England were also helped by Native Americans. People of great religious faith, the Plymouth settlers had no doubt that these Native Americans, named Squanto and Samoset, were *"instruments from God"* sent to help them.

A miracle plant

The people of Plymouth told the story of how the Native Americans *"showed them how to set their corn and where to take fish."* Like the people of Jamestown, they soon realized that their future depended on the new farming skills that the Native Americans taught them.

The Native Americans grew a variety of foods, such as peas, beans, squashes, and pumpkins. But there was one plant above all others that provided the newcomers with enough to eat: corn (maize), or "Indian corn" as the settlers called it. The corn was planted in small mounds of earth. Fish was sometimes added as a fertilizer to make the soil richer, but the corn would grow in almost any kind of soil. It would even grow

The plant shown here is Indian corn, or maize. This crop made the difference between life and death for the first European settlers, who came to rely on it for food.

between trees on land that had not been completely cleared. It provided food for the settlers and for their animals; not even the stalks were wasted. The settlers were delighted with their miracle plant. *"The abundant growth of corn shows this country to be a wonder,"* exclaimed one writer.

Here a kitchen from colonial days has been restored at the governor's palace in Williamsburg, Virginia. Compare it with your kitchen at home. What differences do you notice?

"A store of good things to eat"

The settlers had to grow everything they needed. In some colonies they worked together, sharing the land. But there were sometimes quarrels, with one person accusing another of being lazy. Gradually land was distributed among the settlers, with a certain amount going to each family. One man who watched this happen in Virginia was quite certain that everyone worked harder under the new arrangement: *"They did not work so much in a week as now they do in a day."* Many people shared his view. And there was much hard work to be done. In the days of the first settlers, each family, down to the smallest children, had to labor in the fields. Their efforts were at last rewarded, and they produced *"a store of good things to eat."* Days were set aside for prayers thanking God once the harvest was safely collected. The first "thanksgiving" was held by the Pilgrims at Plymouth in 1621. The custom continues to this day.

The Meetinghouse

The center of many settlements in New England was the meetinghouse, which was both a Puritan church and a community meeting place. John Winthrop (1588–1649), first governor of Massachusetts, recorded how the settlers' work began:

The congregation began the meetinghouse at Boston. They gave their money freely.

A place to pray

Many of the first settlers in New England were Puritans, members of the Protestant Church who believed in leading strict, hardworking lives. An account of New England's early history, which was written by Cotton Mather (1633–1728), a preacher who lived at the time, will show you how important religion was in the Puritan way of life. Mather described the settlers' journey by sea to their new home in America: *"The ministers and passengers served God morning and night, reading and explaining the word of God and singing his praise."* As soon as they reached land, these newcomers turned their thoughts to building a meetinghouse for religious services.

Mud, thatch, timber

Meetinghouses were simple buildings, for a plain style fitted the Puritans' religious beliefs. *"A homely thing like a barn"*—this was how one man described the meetinghouse near his home. At Hingham, in Massachusetts, you can still see one of these early meetinghouses. It was built in 1681, when local people contributed more than £400 (about $600) for the

For their religious worship, the first European settlers had buildings of great simplicity—a far cry from later meetinghouses like this one.

Fine public buildings, like those on the street in Philadelphia shown here, were built by the settlers when they had time. But for the first to arrive, architecture was a rough and ready affair. The first meetinghouses and churches had to be built hastily, out of simple materials.

construction work. At this time, a craftsman might be paid about two shillings (15 cents) for a day's work, so you can see that the people of Hingham were prepared to devote a very great sum of money to building a place of worship.

The meetinghouse at Hingham was built using massive timbers. These formed the framework for the building. The roofing was made of thatch. Other meetinghouses were still plainer and simpler, such as the "Mud Wall" meetinghouse built in Boston, Massachusetts, in the 1630s. This had no windows or heating. As time went by, meetinghouses were often made bigger, to make room for more people. These were sometimes more permanent and imposing buildings made of brick.

But no matter how they were built, all meetinghouses had one very important feature in common: The interior was very bare. There was no place for furnishings that would distract people's attention from the words of prayer and worship. There was a pulpit for the preacher, a table for communion services, and hard wooden pews for seating, but nothing else was thought to be really important.

A place for laws and soldiers

Meetinghouses were not used only for worship. A great number of community activities went on inside. New laws were posted on the meetinghouse door so that

Many of the first New England colonies were settled by Puritans. They were strict Protestants who frowned on people whose religious beliefs were different from their own. In time, more tolerant feelings about religion developed, particularly in places such as Pennsylvania. Here, William Penn, the founder of Pennsylvania, talks to the Native Americans.

people could read them. Meetings and discussions took place there. Among the most important of these were meetings of the courts that ruled the New England colonies. Sometimes weapons and gunpowder for local soldiers were kept in the meetinghouse. This could have unexpected results—John Winthrop noted one such story in his diary. This was the tale of how one of the preachers in Massachusetts accidentally set fire to the meeting house while he was *"drying a little gunpowder."* This happened *"in the new meeting-house, which was thatched, but the thatch only blacked a little,"* Winthrop tells us.

Taking care of the meetinghouse was itself a community affair. At the meetinghouse in Southampton, New York, for example, each family took turns making a fire to keep the congregation warm during services. Above all, the meetinghouse was a place for friends and neighbors. Here newcomers got to know each other and began to feel at home in a new land.

THE TOBACCO FIELD

A day's work in the tobacco field comes to life in the pages of a diary written in the 1700s:

My tobacco seems very good. Our harvest yesterday was so great that although all hands began at twelve, we could not get it all out of the ground before the rain came.

Worms, weeds, weather

These words were written by a wealthy man named Landon Carter. Landon Carter grew a great deal of tobacco on his plantations in Virginia, and he carefully recorded all the work that was done there. Reading his diary is a very good way to find out about tobacco and how it was grown.

First of all, the farmer sowed the tobacco seed. When the seed began to come up, it was time to plant it out in the fields, in soil piled up to form little heaps. Tobacco plants grew well in any kind of ground, but they had to be well tended. On Landon Carter's estates—and on many other American plantations in the south— this work was done by slaves from Africa. The ground had to be hoed and weeded, and pests such as hornworm had to be picked off the plants. All these tasks were done by

Growing the tobacco plant gave many colonies the opportunity to make money.

19

hand. Carter's diary tells us that growing tobacco meant constant worries about worms, weeds, and weather. *"Goodbye tobacco,"* he wrote gloomily on one occasion when the weather was especially bad.

Despite Carter's gloom, his tobacco often did very well. This meant more work cutting and harvesting. Then the tobacco had to be "cured"—hung up to dry in the air. Finally the leaves and stalks were separated, and the tobacco was packed away in casks. At last it was ready to be sold.

The tobacco craze

The Native Americans had grown tobacco for many years. But to the people of Europe, tobacco was a new discovery. It was first shipped to Europe by merchants

Gentlemen in England smoking their clay pipes. Tobacco became very popular in Europe, and the crops that the American settlers grew were much in demand.

during the 1500s, and smoking rapidly became popular. Some people were so enthusiastic about tobacco, they declared that it promoted good health. One Englishman, named Thomas Harriot, described how tobacco could be *"dried and turned into powder"* and then burned, to produce smoke. The smoke, he explained, was a kind of medicine. People who breathed it *"improved in health."* Doctors today would not agree with him! Most people in the 1500s and 1600s, however, smoked tobacco simply for pleasure.

Something to trade

The people of Europe were very eager for the first settlers in America to grow tobacco for them. Many of the settlers were just as pleased with the arrangement. There was an important reason for this: cash. The settlers depended on Europe for all sorts of supplies that they could not yet provide for themselves—from certain sorts of foodstuffs to furniture, from cloth to cattle. *"Loving father, I would ask you that you would send me butter and four or*

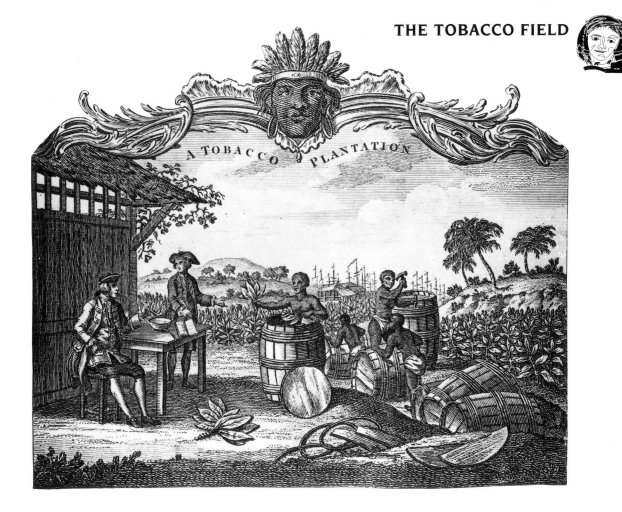

A TOBACCO PLANTATION

five yards of cloth to make some clothes," one newly arrived settler wrote to his father in England. Many requests like this were sent across the ocean. To pay for all that they needed, the settlers needed money—or something to trade. For many of the colonies, tobacco was the answer.

Virginia was one of the most important tobacco-growing areas. At the beginning of the seventeenth century, Captain John Smith recorded how the first settlers at Jamestown, excited by their new crop, planted it *"in the marketplace, streets, and all other spare places."* By 1700, the people of the British colonies of mainland America were growing more than 12,500 tons of tobacco each year. Most of this was sold to Britain. Growing tobacco was most easily done on a large scale, involving lots of workers. Planters who could farm in this way became very prosperous.

At work on an American tobacco plantation. Plantations were run by slave labor. Here, slaves are busy packing the crop into barrels.

21

THE HUNTING GROUND

Hunting wild animals for food helped the Native Americans in their struggle for survival in their environment. A settler in Maryland in the 1630s described the hunt:

Their weapons are a bow and bundle of arrows, feathered with turkey feathers, and headed with deer horn, glass or flints. They daily catch partridge, deer, turkeys, and squirrels.

Living with nature

The Native Americans hunted with traditional weapons. The arrival of European settlers brought change. What type of weapon do the men in this canoe carry?

These words, written by a priest named Andrew White, tell us a great deal about the Native Americans' way of life. This lifestyle was simple by the settlers' standards, yet the Native Americans had developed quite complex skills to allow them to feed and support themselves. These included fishing, hunting, gathering food plants that grew wild, and growing foods such as corn, beans, and squash.

The food and activities of the year often formed a pattern that depended on the wildlife. Where animals were abundant, the hunters followed. You can see this pattern in the activities of the Micmac people, who lived in the area that is known as Nova Scotia and New Brunswick today. The Micmacs hunted seals in January, then moose, otter, and caribou; in spring and summer they went fishing on the coast; and in the autumn they returned to their hunting, this time for elk and beaver. In January the pattern began all over again.

This was a way of life that involved a great deal of

When they reached America, many early European settlers thought that they had come to an empty country. In reality, the land had been settled, farmed, and hunted on for many hundreds of years by Native American peoples.

knowledge about wild animals and birds and their habits. Often too, it meant being on the move, traveling great distances as wild animals were tracked in the hunting grounds.

A wild land?

The first Europeans to arrive in North America found it very different from their homelands. They were used to carefully tended fields of crops and grassy meadows grazed by cattle and sheep. In America they found great stretches of forest, as well as fearsome beasts they had never met before. Animals such as black bears, alligators, and panthers, for example, worried settlers in the Carolinas. One man described how he would go to sleep at night there only to be *"awakened with the most hideous noise"* as the animals nearby began to howl.

The settlers felt that they had arrived in a wild land, and they planned to change it. Cotton Mather put forward this point of view at the beginning of the eighteenth century: *"Why should we allow whole lands, profitable for man, to lie waste without improvement?"*

23

Different views of one land

The Native Americans looked at the land and saw it as a place where they could live. The settlers looked at it and saw a wilderness that had to be tamed before they could live there. The two points of view were completely different, and they were to cause much bitterness. As explorers and settlers from Europe claimed land in the New World as their own, few felt that they should pay attention to the way that the Native Americans used the land. *"They do not use even one fourth of the land,"* said one settler. But he was wrong. Like other settlers, he simply did not understand *how* the Native Americans used the land.

Spot the hunters! Some Native Americans hunted deer by disguising themselves with deer-skins, so that they could come very close to the deer without startling them. If you look at the "deer" on the left of the picture, you will see that they are hunters in disguise.

Living together

The Native Americans greeted the newcomers with friendly curiosity at first. They were eager to trade, exchanging the furs obtained by their hunters for goods brought by the settlers—metal ware, guns, alcohol. All these were new to the Native Americans. But as the settlers began to take the land that had been used for hunting and farming by the different American tribes, the relationship became hostile. Struggles between the settlers and the Native Americans broke out in many places.

THE STREET

The work of laying out a new settlement can be seen through the eyes of William Bradford (1590–1657), one of the Pilgrims and later governor of Plymouth colony:

We went on shore, some to cut wood, some to saw, some to carry. We divided the plot of land to build our town and agreed that every man should build his own house.

Building a new world

William Bradford wrote about the life of the first settlers at Plymouth colony in New England during the 1620s. But the story he told was true of conditions anywhere a new colony was set up: *"They had now no friends to welcome them, no house nor towns to go to."* The first to arrive had to turn their hands to building, working to make homes for their families.

The first houses to be built were usually simple, the walls made with a timber frame and the roofs covered in thatch. Bit by bit, as more newcomers arrived, more houses went up and the land nearby was planted with crops. So the settlements of America grew.

Numbers grow

The first great rush of newcomers moving to America took place during the 1630s and 1640s. So many people left England, for instance, that the government began to worry. Allowing *"such swarms to go out of England*

A visitor to New York in 1673 would have been greeted by this view. Farmland and countryside ringed the city.

Nieuw-Amsterdam onlangs Nieuw jorck genaemt.
ende hernomen bij de Nederlanders op den 24 Aug: 1673

will upset trade," fretted one writer of the time. You can see what he meant by "swarms" of people if you look at the numbers who arrived in some of the colonies. The story of Plymouth colony is a good example. In 1630 it was home to 300 people. By 1640, 3,000 people lived there. The number of newcomers was growing rapidly. During the 1700s there was another great wave of newcomers to the British colonies. This time they came not just from Britain, but from many other parts of Europe, too—Germany, the Netherlands, Ireland, France, Scandinavia.

The rise in numbers meant that American towns, especially in the colonies ruled by the British, grew quickly. Philadelphia in Pennsylvania soon became the largest town in America. In 1760, more than 23,000 people lived there. Fifteen years later, it had twice as many inhabitants.

This house, in Dedham, Massachusetts, takes us right back to the days of the early European settlers. The house dates from 1636. This type of building is called a "frame" house.

Fair streets and public buildings

People arriving in America during the 1700s would have found that conditions had changed in the short time since William Bradford had written about the early days at Plymouth colony. Many settlements along the coast were developing into busy towns. In 1708 a visitor to Charleston, in South Carolina, described the way this town was growing: *"It is a market town. There are several fair streets in the town. There is a public library and a free school has been talked of for some time."* When these words were written, about 6,000 people lived in Charleston. Yet just 20 years before there had been only 300 inhabitants. At this time brambles and bushes grew in many of the streets, and hogs wandered about town as they pleased. You can see from these descriptions that change was very rapid in many American towns.

Hustle-bustle and business

The more people who came to live in the towns and settlements of America, the busier everyday life became. There were many things to arrange, from keeping the streets clean and making sure that stray animals—like the hogs in Charleston—did no damage, to choosing men to set up law courts and govern the people. As the towns grew, it became possible for the settlers to earn a living by working as craftsmen, or by setting up shop and selling their wares. In the little town of Boston, Massachusetts, for example, it was a very special day when *"John Cogan, merchant, set up the first shop"* in the 1630s. From small beginnings, Boston became a bustling harbor town. Boatbuilders, butchers, brewers, carpenters, black-smiths, innkeepers, and many other merchants and craftsmen did well there. In other American towns, too, this was a time of growth and prosperity.

The town of Concord, Massachusetts, in 1775. You can see soldiers ready for battle. Ideas about politics and freedom were developing rapidly at this time, and by 1775 many people were preparing to fight Britain to win independence.

THE CHURCH

I n town and country alike, the church was close to the heart of local life. The words of a man named Robert Beverley, who lived in the eighteenth century, record this fact for us:

They have in each parish a convenient church, built either of timber, brick or stone.

From sailcloth and wood, to elegance in brick

The churches of the first settlers, built just 100 years before Beverley wrote his account, were very different from the "convenient" buildings he described. The newcomers were happy just to have a shelter where they could worship God, no matter what it looked like. An eyewitness description of one of the settlers' first religious services makes this clear: *"We did hang a sail on the trees to shade us from the sun. Our walls were rails of wood nailed to trees. This was our first church."*

By the 1700s, the British colonies in America were becoming settled and prosperous. This could be seen in

This picture shows a group of Christians called Quakers. Quakers were persecuted in Europe, but many found freedom in America. The colony of Pennsylvania was founded in 1681 by a famous Quaker named William Penn.

the care and attention given to the appearance of new church buildings. Churches in towns such as New York, Boston, and Philadelphia were based on the up-to-date style of building made popular by the English architect Sir Christopher Wren (1631–1723). Elegant brick-built churches like these were a long way from the early churches of sailcloth and wood.

Religion with freedom

In Europe it was expected that the people of each country would follow the religion of their rulers. For example, if the king or queen was a Protestant Christian, the people would have to accept Protestant beliefs. This sometimes caused much resentment, and many of the first settlers came to America because they wanted to be free to choose their own religious beliefs. Benjamin Franklin (1706–1790), a great American writer and diplomat, explained that his father had left England for this reason. In the New World, said Franklin, his family *"expected to enjoy their religion with freedom."*

The faith of the first colonies

Many of the first colonies were founded by people for whom religion was very important. In New England, most colonies were founded by people of Puritan belief. The colony of Pennsylvania was settled in the 1680s in accordance with the ideas of a man named William Penn, who was a Quaker. The founders of these colonies wanted to create a place where people whose religious belief was attacked in Europe could worship freely. In areas of North America where Spain had interests, such as California, Roman Catholic missionaries carried out religious work.

Early European visitors to America were eager to record all they saw. The artist who painted this picture was just such a traveler. His name was John White. This is his picture of a Native American burial house. Some settlers were interested in converting Native Americans, others let them be.

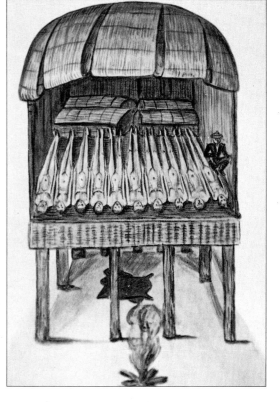

Deep religious faith was the driving force for many early settlers. Building a church, like this one, was one of their first priorities when they established a new settlement.

From religious quarrels to religious peace

The earliest settlers did not intend to allow complete religious freedom. It was not thought possible that people with different religious views could live together, and so the leaders of each colony expected to lay down what religious beliefs people should hold – even though they had left Europe to get away from arrangements like this. When there were quarrels about religion in New England, for instance, the Puritan leaders were quick to punish those who disagreed with them. In 1635, a preacher named Roger Williams was forced to leave Plymouth colony because of a dispute about religion. Williams founded a new colony at Rhode Island. Here he established a church where God was worshipped according to the ideas of a group of Christians called Baptists, and he encouraged tolerance in religious matters.

Gradually opinions began to change. The Quaker colony of Pennsylvania was one of the first places where new ideas took root. Here, in 1701, a special privilege was granted to the inhabitants. Everyone who believed in *"one almighty God"* was to be allowed to live there in peace. This meant that all Christian believers would be allowed to worship freely—not just Quakers. This idea of "religious tolerance" soon became an important part of the American way of life.

THE COLLEGE

I n the 1660s, servants of King Charles II of England (reigned 1660–1685) visited Massachusetts in New England. They reported on what they saw. In the town of Cambridge, it was the college that impressed them:

In Cambridge they have a wooden college, and in the yard, a brick building for the Indians. They said they had three or more Indians at school there.

Faith and knowledge

There are many clues that tell us how the first settlers in America felt about education. Many people, especially in the New England settlements, believed that it was vital for children—and adults—to be given an education. They thought of education above all as a way of deepening their religious faith. They wanted to be able to read so that they could read the Bible, and they wanted good schools and colleges so that men could be trained as ministers. Many of the settlers also hoped to teach the Native Americans about Christianity. For these reasons, setting up a college was an important priority for the people of the colonies. One writer put the settlers' feelings like this: *"One of the things we longed for was to advance learning."*

This self portrait by Thomas Smith shows a cultured man. This sense of culture and learning was reinforced at colleges such as Harvard, where Smith lived.

The first college

The college at Cambridge described at the beginning of this chapter was the first to be built by the settlers.

One of its most important aims was to train men to serve as Puritan ministers. The college was begun in 1636, just six years after the first Puritan settlers arrived in Massachusetts. This was quick work indeed. It soon came to be called Harvard College, taking the name of a scholar named John Harvard (1607–1638). Harvard had helped the new college by leaving it books and money in his will when he died. Like other Puritan leaders in Massachusetts, Harvard had studied at Emmanuel College, which was part of the college of Cambridge in England. When these men came to set up a college in America, they thought of the way that life and study had been arranged for the students at Emmanuel, and they decided to use some of these ideas. There are still close links between students at Harvard and students at Emmanuel today.

Getting an education

Harvard was the first college, but others soon followed. In Virginia, the College of William and Mary was founded in 1693, while Yale was founded in

Harvard, America's oldest university. The college was named after John Harvard, a scholar from England. Together with 32 others John Harvard came to America in the 1630s in search of religious freedom.

Connecticut in 1701. By 1769 there were nine colleges in America, each founded by a religious group.

In each college, the students' life followed a similar pattern. There was much hard work to do. The day started with prayers at sunrise, and lasted until it was time for supper, prayers, and private study at night. There were lectures in the morning and debates in the afternoon. Students lived in the college. They had to pay for their classes and for all the everyday things they needed, from meals to firewood and candles. Students and staff took their meals together in a great hall. There were sometimes grumbles about the food. *"Nothing but porridge and puddings,"* complained students at Harvard in 1639.

Only a small number of people went to college – and these were all young men, for women were not thought to need such an education. But many people were given a basic education at school. Very early laws in New England ordered all towns to set up schools where children could be taught to read and write. The people of Boston were some of the first settlers to set up a school for local children.

The College of William and Mary in Virginia was founded in 1693. Botany and zoology were popular subjects to study, as we can see from the picture here.

THE POST OFFICE

Here a famous American who helped to set up a postal service in the 1700s describes a place in town that was always busy—the post office:

Bradford kept the post office. He had a good opportunity of hearing all the news.

Setting up a postal service

Almost as soon as the first Europeans settled in the New World, they began to think of setting up a postal service. Letters to and from Europe were sent across the ocean by ship. But how were letters to be sent from one place to another in America itself? There were many problems to overcome. The problem of transportation was one of the most difficult.

At first there were no roads in the new colonies, only hunting trails and the tracks made by buffaloes and other animals. Thick woods and dense undergrowth had to be cleared before roads could be built. This meant that waterways often provided the easiest transport. George Washington, the first president of the United States (1732–1799), tells a story that shows how waterways were used as highways by the early settlers. *"The country along the Potomac River was settled with many families,"* he wrote. *"Visits were made by row-boats."* Setting up a postal service in these conditions would have been very difficult. But little by little, the problem of transportation was overcome. A network of roads was laid. This made travel by land easier. And where there were roads, horses and riders or stage-coaches carrying mail could go too. Gradually arrangements were made so that mail could be sent from one colony to another on a regular basis. Improvements were made to make the service as

speedy as possible. Much of this work was directed by the energetic post office official whose words began this chapter. His name was Benjamin Franklin.

As the road network developed, people and mail were moved between cities in stagecoaches like the "Flying Machine."

Post office and meeting place

The post office was a hive of activity. Many post office owners worked at a whole range of jobs, and so the post office also served as a printer's workshop, a general store—even a newspaper office. This meant that customers who came to collect their mail had the opportunity to do all sorts of other things while they were at the post office. They could buy almost anything, from newspapers to medicine. They could also place an order for printing, or just catch up with local gossip. There was always time for a chat with the person who ran the post office and with other customers. You can see why Bradford, the postmaster described by Benjamin Franklin at the beginning of this chapter, heard all the news.

Books and pamphlets were printed on a printing press such as this in colonial times.

Passing on the news

Printing a newspaper as well as running a post office seemed like a good business opportunity to many post office owners. Postmaster Bradford did this in Philadelphia, Pennsylvania, for example. Newspapers like Bradford's were very different from today's papers. Many were published only once a week. They covered four pages and carried advertisements, notices of when ships would arrive in local ports, letters, speeches made by powerful officials in the colonies, and reports of important events in Europe. The first American newspaper was called the *Boston News-Letter*. It began in 1704 and was printed by a postmaster named John Campbell.

Newspapers had an important part to play in spreading ideas. This was especially true in the British colonies in the middle of the eighteenth century, when there were arguments about how the colonies should be ruled. A growing number of people felt that Britain was using its power over America in the wrong way, and American newspapers carried many articles about the problem. Some of the most famous were called the "Farmer's Letters." They were written in the 1760s by a farmer and lawyer from Pennsylvania named John Dickinson.

THE FORT

An eyewitness account of how a fort was built was written by an American soldier in the 1700s:

I hurried to complete the fort. We built with logs, chest high. There was no roof. The fort was one hundred feet square and surrounded by a ditch and fence.

The fort was at Great Meadows, Pennsylvania. The soldier was George Washington, who was soon to become a great American leader.

A place of defense

The settlers in America were anxious to build forts. They provided a place of defense, where a band of local men could keep watch and alert their neighbors if danger threatened. Building a fort and making arrangements for settlers to turn soldier and stand guard were among the first tasks in most colonies. *"We shall fortify ourselves in a short time,"* wrote one early settler in New England. If the worst happened, the fort was somewhere for the settlers to hide from enemy attack.

A fort coming under attack from enemy forces. Guns and cannons played a vital role in actions like this.

Holding the frontier

Forts also played an important part in the dramatic story of exploration. This was especially true in the eighteenth century. This was a time when there was growing enthusiasm to explore the interior of America, to the west of the areas on the Atlantic coast where the British colonies had been established. Settlers in Virginia were particularly eager to push west and stake a claim to land there.

The drive westward brought conflict—not only with the Native Americans who lived in this area, but also between people from different European backgrounds. The British and French were bitter enemies. They fought many wars in Europe, and their rivalry boiled over in America. Both the British settlers and the French wanted power in lands in the west of America; and each side used forts to try to get what it wanted. From their bases in Canada to the north and in New Orleans in the south, the French built a string of forts along the great waterways linking the North and South. These included St Louis (Missouri) in 1682, and Detroit (Michigan) in 1701. Then, in 1753, forts were built along the Ohio River, too. The English settlers responded in

Training an army, and providing arms, equipment, food, medical supplies, and pay, caused many difficulties for the American colonies when they began their fight for independence. Here you can see the British armed forces training in America. The British, too, faced problems.

the same way, building forts such as the one at Great Meadows, described at the beginning of this chapter. Forts like these were built as centers of exploration and as trading posts. Above all, they were strongholds showing where each side staked its claim to land and power along the frontier, which was continually being redrawn.

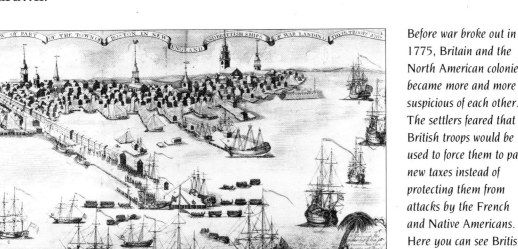

Before war broke out in 1775, Britain and the North American colonies became more and more suspicious of each other. The settlers feared that British troops would be used to force them to pay new taxes instead of protecting them from attacks by the French and Native Americans. Here you can see British troops landing at Boston in 1768.

Uneasy times

The settlers who came to America knew that they faced many dangers. They feared attacks from the Native Americans. They also knew that if war broke out among the countries of Europe, then war between the British, French and Spanish in America was likely to follow. These fears became reality on many occasions. In 1675, for example, the New England colonies fought a fierce war known as King Philip's War against three Native American tribes: the Narragansett, the Nipmuck, and the Wampanoag. A few years later, war in Europe brought fighting to America in King William's War. This was a contest between the British and the French, each aided by their Native American allies. Forts were important in times of war like these.

THE HARBOR

The first Europeans to live in America arrived and settled on the Atlantic coast. They found many good sites for ports and harbors. Here a visitor to South Carolina in the 1680s describes the ships he saw in the harbor at Charleston:

There were sixteen ships which had come to trade. The great number of ships will soon make this a busy town.

Arriving in harbor

The arrival of a ship in harbor was always an exciting event. There were officials on the alert at the dockside, ready to inspect the ships that arrived and to make sure that the right taxes were paid. There were family and friends waiting for new settlers to arrive. And there were crowds waiting to see what useful and exciting

Ships off the port of Charleston in 1739. Trading ships were America's vital link with the world. They brought popular luxuries—such as tea— as well as carrying away goods that the colonies had to sell.

goods from Europe were being unloaded. *"8 pounds of best tea, cinnamon, pepper, currants, raisins, three hats"*—this was the load one settler was impatient to unpack at the harborside. Almost anything could be onboard, from hogs and hens to tea and coffee. When the ship's captain landed his clucking, squealing, interesting-smelling cargo, many things were sold on the spot. At the port of Boston, Massachusetts, some people worried about the crowds. They were troubled about *"people running to the ships and the great price of things."* Their words conjure up a good picture of the busy scene.

Come to trade

Trade was extremely important to the settlers in America. Although the very first settlers to arrive had to struggle to grow enough to eat, farmers were soon producing many different

types of crops. They were eager to trade and they needed a market—people who would buy their produce. In and around the growing towns, businesses were being set up. They, too, wanted customers. Sending food and goods to other countries was a way of selling to many customers. And so the ships that arrived in America's harbors, loaded with things to sell to the settlers, soon sailed back out of harbor, loaded with things to sell to the rest of the world.

Merchants bringing goods to and from the colonies of North America had to pay taxes. Here you can see the Custom House in New York. It was the job of the customs official to see that taxes were paid.

To and from harbor

American goods were sent to many different lands. From the bustling port of Boston, timber was shipped to Spain, while wheat, peas, and corn were sent to the Canary Islands, and foods of all kinds were sent to the Caribbean. One man who lived at the time reported that

Boston Harbor. Dramatic events unfolded here in 1773, when 150 men, disguised as Native Americans, tipped valuable cargoes of tea into the water. This act, which became known as the Boston Tea Party, was a protest against British taxes.

the people of the Caribbean made excellent customers. *"They are so busy planting sugar that they will buy food at very high prices,"* he said. This meant good business for the people of Boston.

Boston was an especially busy port. People from settlements inland traveled there when they had a good crop to sell, or other things to trade. But the story at many other harbors was the same. Settlers from the country brought their goods to the harbor town. There they would be sure to find buyers.

Trade and freedom

The people of the British colonies were not completely free to choose the countries with which they traded. Some of their most valuable products had to be kept for customers in Britain and could not be sold to anyone else. Special laws about this trade were made in London, and because the settlers owed obedience to the British king, they had to obey. One law, called the Navigation Act, which was passed in 1660, set out a list of items that could be sold to Great Britain and nowhere else. The list included sugar, tobacco, cotton, indigo (a plant yielding a purple dye), and ginger. Other laws also tried to control vital parts of the settlers' trade. During the 1700s, these laws began to cause disagreements between the American settlers and the government in Britain.

THE OLD WORLD

The first Europeans who decided to settle in America made a bold move. Life in the "New World" of America was sometimes frightening, and many liked to remember their early days in the "Old World" of Europe. George Washington described this feeling in the 1700s:

Many people had a habit of speaking of England as home. Their attachment to the mother country was very great.

Remembering home

The settlers felt very close to their first homes even though they now lived so far away. The names they chose for their new homes in America tell us about this feeling. Many settlements were named after places in the Old World. There was "Nova Scotia" (New Scotland), "New England," "New Sweden," "New Amsterdam," and "New Netherland," for example. As a sign of loyalty and friendship, settlements were even named after important people from the Old World. Jamestown, one of the first English settlements in Virginia, was named after King James I of England; while Louisiana was named by French settlers in honor of King Louis XIV of France. Many other places were given names that reminded the settlers of home.

This Native American leader was painted during a visit to England in 1710. In Europe, the customs of non-European people were frequently regarded with curiosity at this time.

Like a mother and children

Many people at this time thought of the American colonies as the "children" of the countries of Europe. In the British colonies, laws made by "mother" England were very important. A writer of the time tells us how settlers in Massachusetts asked King James I for *"the power to elect their own officials and make laws for the colony."* But as a sign that the people there relied on England, they were not allowed to make any laws disagreeing with the laws made in London. This story shows that the settlers were not free to rule themselves in any way that they chose.

For many years this caused few problems, but at the time of King George III, who came to the British throne in 1760, the relationship between Britain and America became hostile. Some people in America began to feel that they were being treated unfairly. They complained that Britain interfered too much with the settlers' trade and industry, and they protested new laws and taxes planned by George III's advisers. Many people were very suspicious about the reasons behind these laws and taxes. They feared that they were being treated like children in the worst possible way, and that soon they would have no power over their country's future.

Here we can see the British King, George III. The laws and taxes passed by his advisers brought relations between the Old World and the New World to breaking point.

Growing apart

By the 1760s, feelings were running high, both in Britain and its American colonies. For Britain, money was a pressing problem. Expensive wars had been fought in many parts of the globe, such as the "French and Indian War" of 1756–1763 (called the Seven Years War by people in Europe). Now Britain wanted to raise money by taxing the American colonies. The colonies

In this picture the French claim the lower Mississippi and call it Louisiana after their king, Louis XIV. France lost out to Britain in its search for colonies in the Americas.

reacted angrily. One woman wrote a poem about a tax on the most popular drink of the time: tea. Calling herself a "Daughter of Liberty," she declared that it was better to go without all sorts of good things, like tea, than to pay an unjust tax. "Rather than freedom we'll part with our tea," she wrote. Many people felt like this. Customers banded together and agreed not to buy tea if it was taxed. Even the students at Harvard College joined in.

Other people feared that Britain meant to stop them exploring lands to the west, which were traditionally used as hunting grounds by the Native Americans. For reasons like these, many settlers' feelings of loyalty toward Britain began to weaken. In 1776, the beginning of a new era dawned and the British colonies declared themselves independent: free from rule by Britain and the Old World.

GLOSSARY

Ally (plural, allies)   A supporter.

Architect   Someone who designs buildings.

Assembly   A meeting of men who decided how a colony should be ruled.

Baptist   A Christian who believes that being baptized is especially important. Being baptized makes a person a member of the Christian Church, and is a sign that he or she truly believes in Jesus Christ.

Blacksmith   Someone who works with metal, especially iron.

Colony   A place ruled by people from another land.

Empire   Colonies ruled by one country.

Governor   Someone who led the government of a colony.

Independent   Free. Not ruled by another person or country.

Meetinghouse   A Puritan church and gathering place.

Missionary   Someone who aims to persuade other people to follow his or her religious beliefs.

Native Americans   People who lived in America when settlers from Europe arrived. The settlers called these people "Indians."

New World   The name given to America by the people of Europe.

Old World   The name given to Europe.

Pilgrims   The group of settlers who sailed to Plymouth, New England, in a ship called the *Mayflower* in 1620. They likened their journey to a new land to a religious journey or pilgrimage.

Plantation   A large farm.

Protestant   A Christian who does not accept the teaching of the Pope, and who is not a member of the Roman Catholic Church.

Pulpit   A raised step where a minister stands to preach in a church or meeting house.

Puritan   A Protestant Christian with very strict beliefs and way of life.

Quaker   A Christian who worships God in a very simple way. The Quakers were greatly influenced by the ideas of a man named George Fox.

Religious tolerance   Allowing people with different religious beliefs to live peacefully together.

Scurvy   An illness caused by lack of vitamin C in the diet.

Settlement   A town or village built by people coming to live in a new place.

Settler   Someone who goes to live in a new land.

Tax   Money paid to the government.

FURTHER READING

Alden R Carter, *Colonial Wars: Clashes in the Wilderness*, Franklin Watts, 1993.

Dennis B Fradin, *The Thirteen Colonies*. Children's Press, 1988.

Carter, Smith, ed., *Daily Life: A Sourcebook on Colonial America*, Millbrook Press, 1991.

Laurel Van der Linde, *The Devil in Salem Village: The Story of the Salem Witchcraft Trials*, Millbrook Press, 1992.

John F Warner, *Colonial American Home Life*, Franklin Watts, 1993.

G Clifton Wisler, *This New Land*, Walker & Co, 1987.

INDEX